Birds Coloring Book

Realistic Adult Coloring Book, Advanced Birds Coloring Book for Adults

Realistic Animal Coloring Book: Vol 6

by Amanda Davenport

ISBN-13: 978-1530585892

ISBN-10: 1530585899

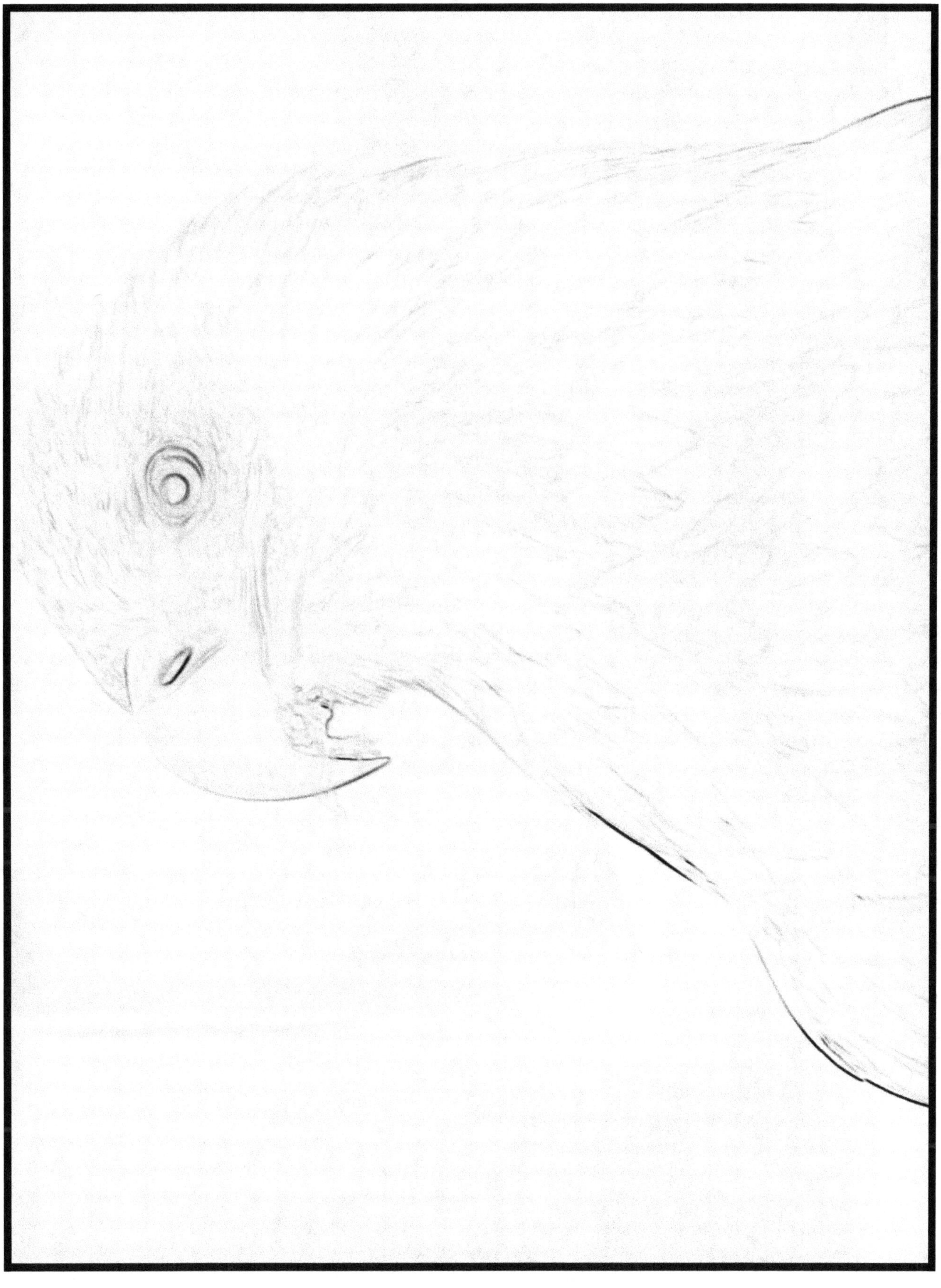

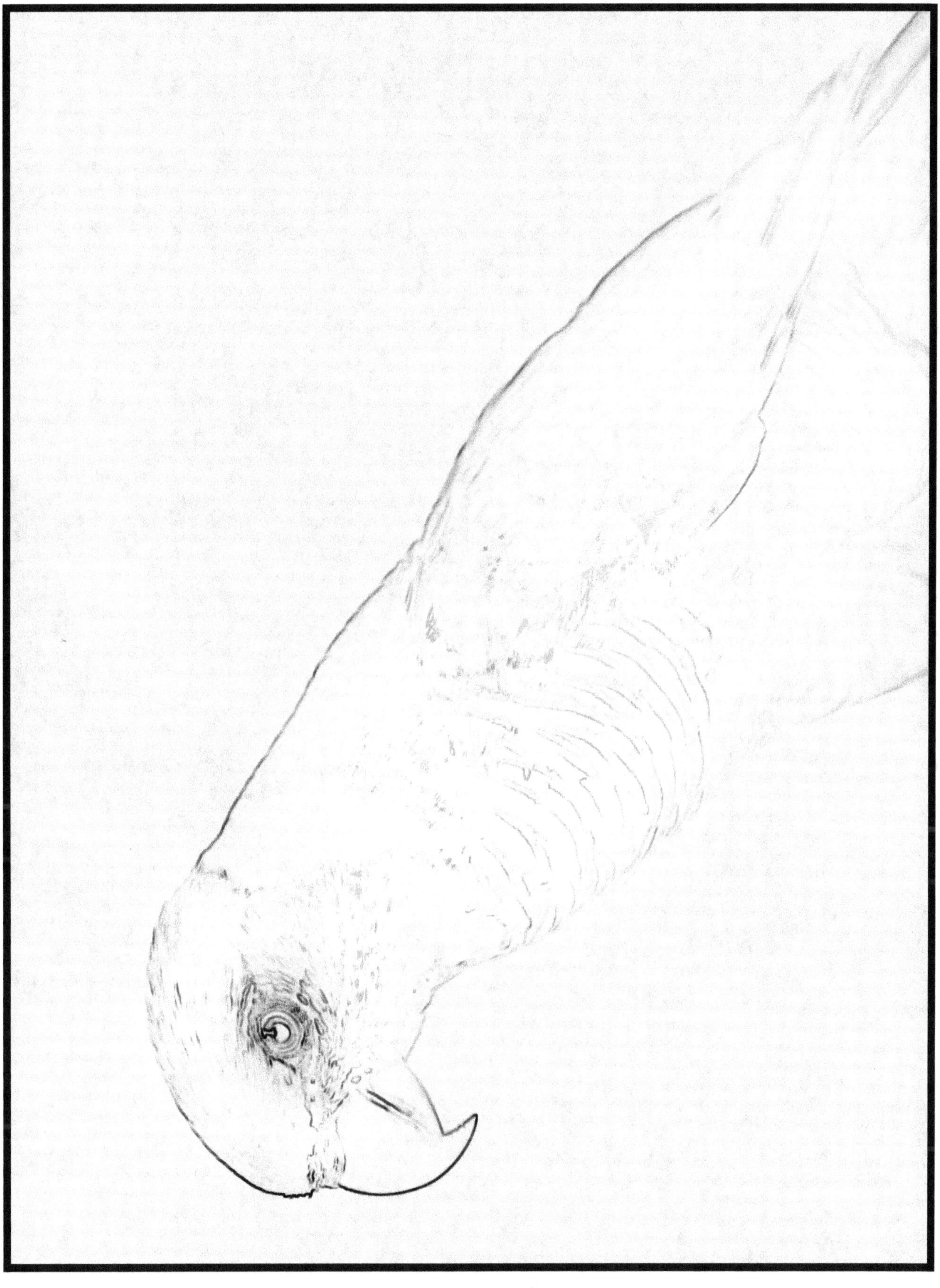

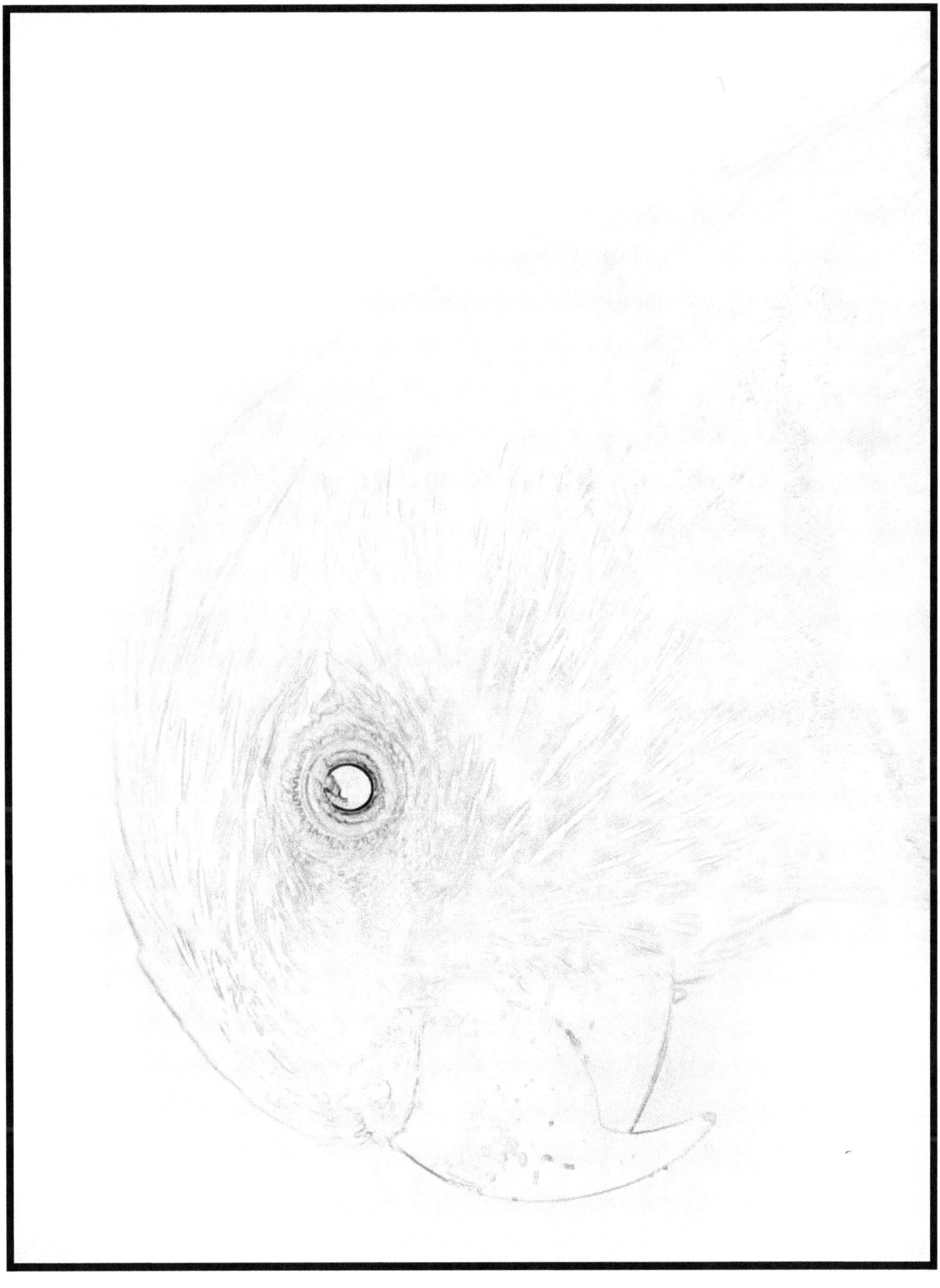

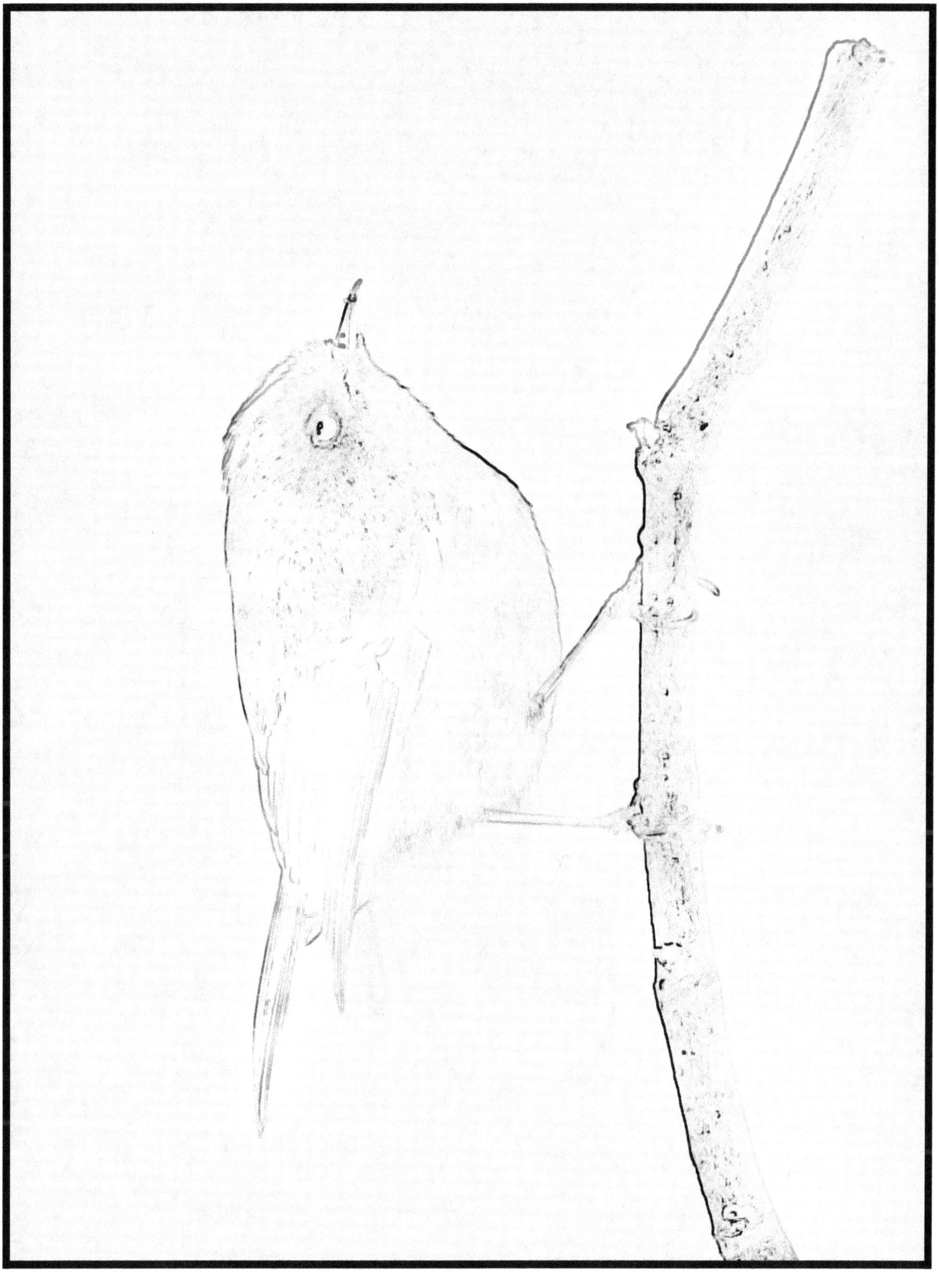

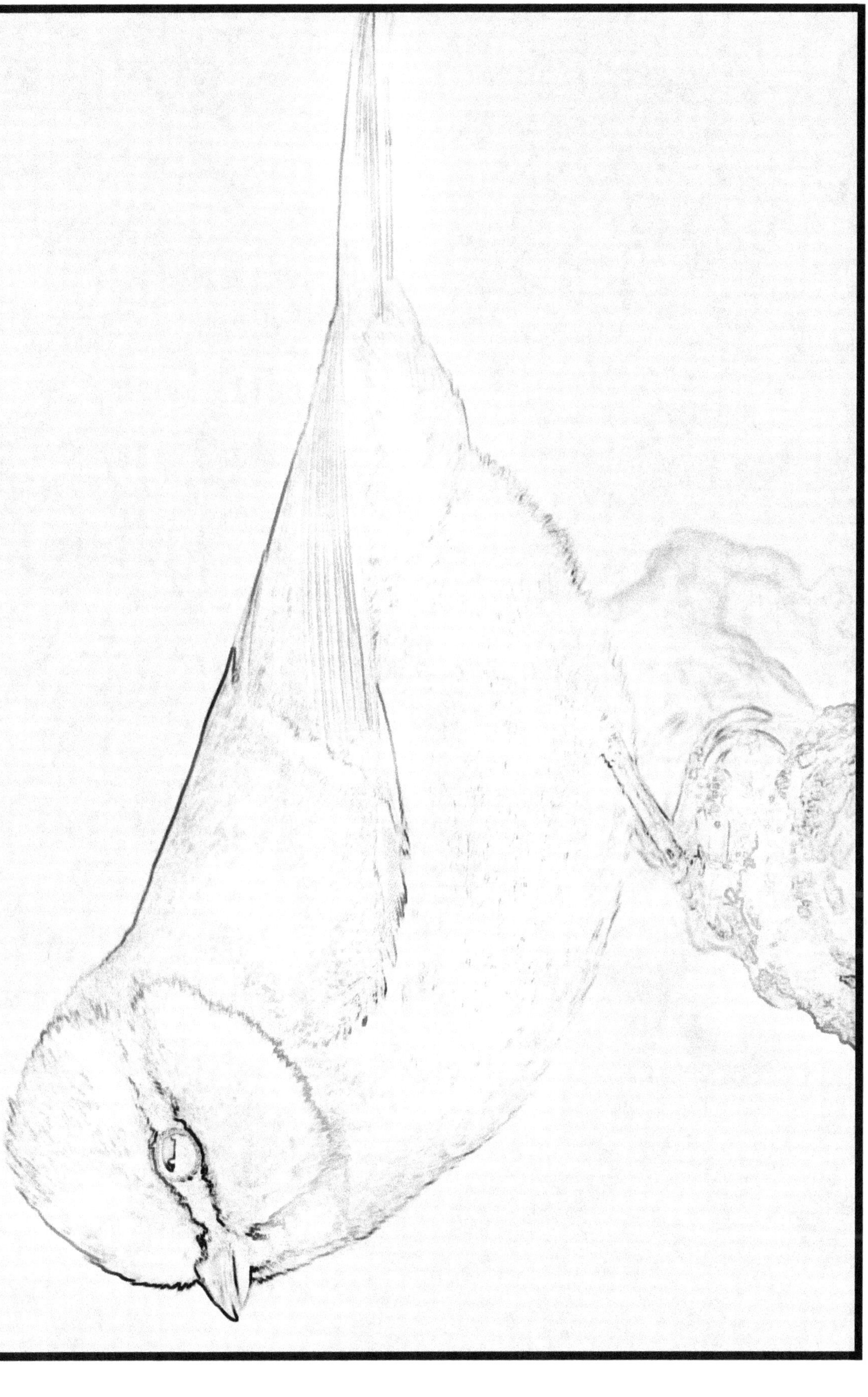

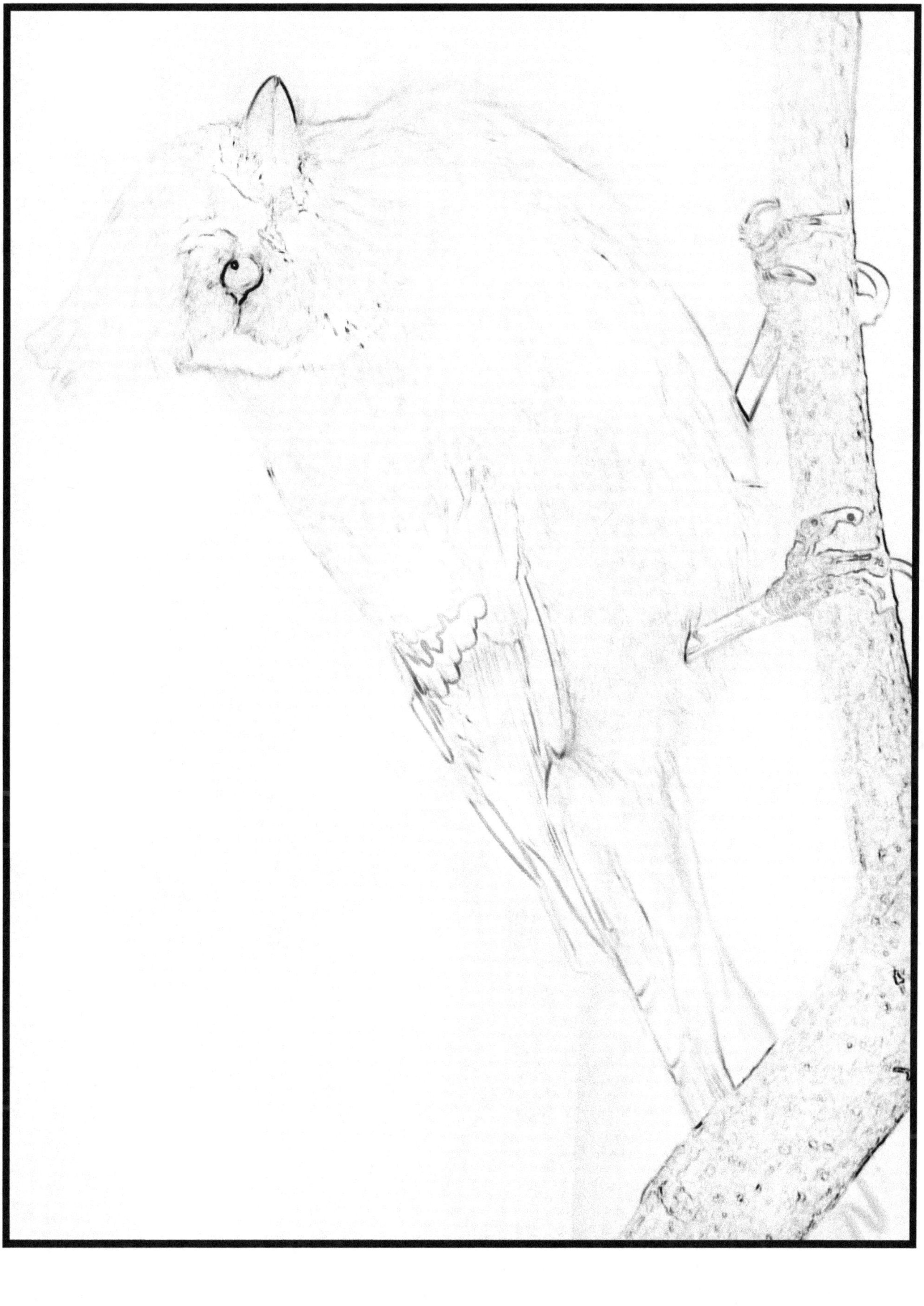

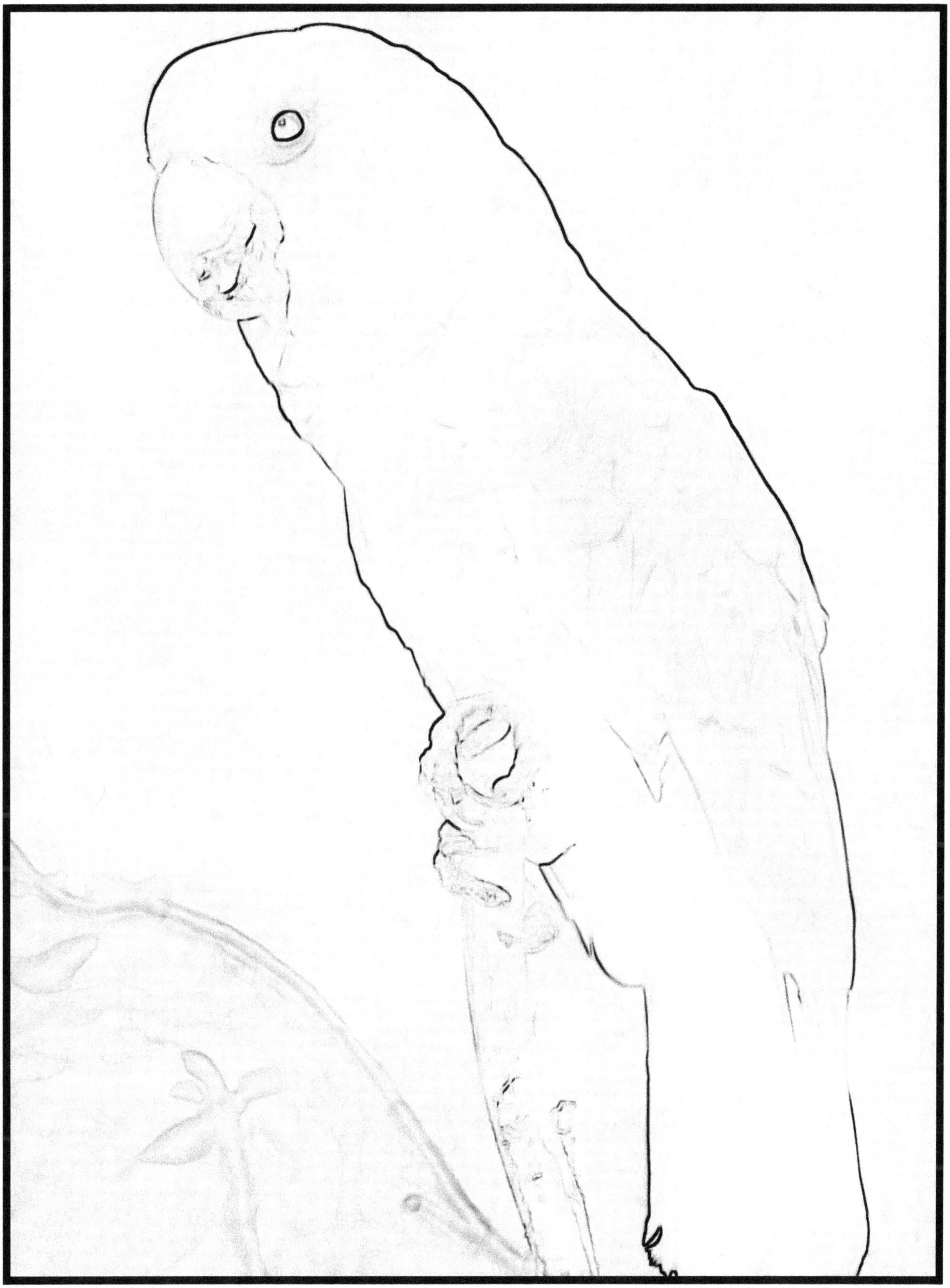

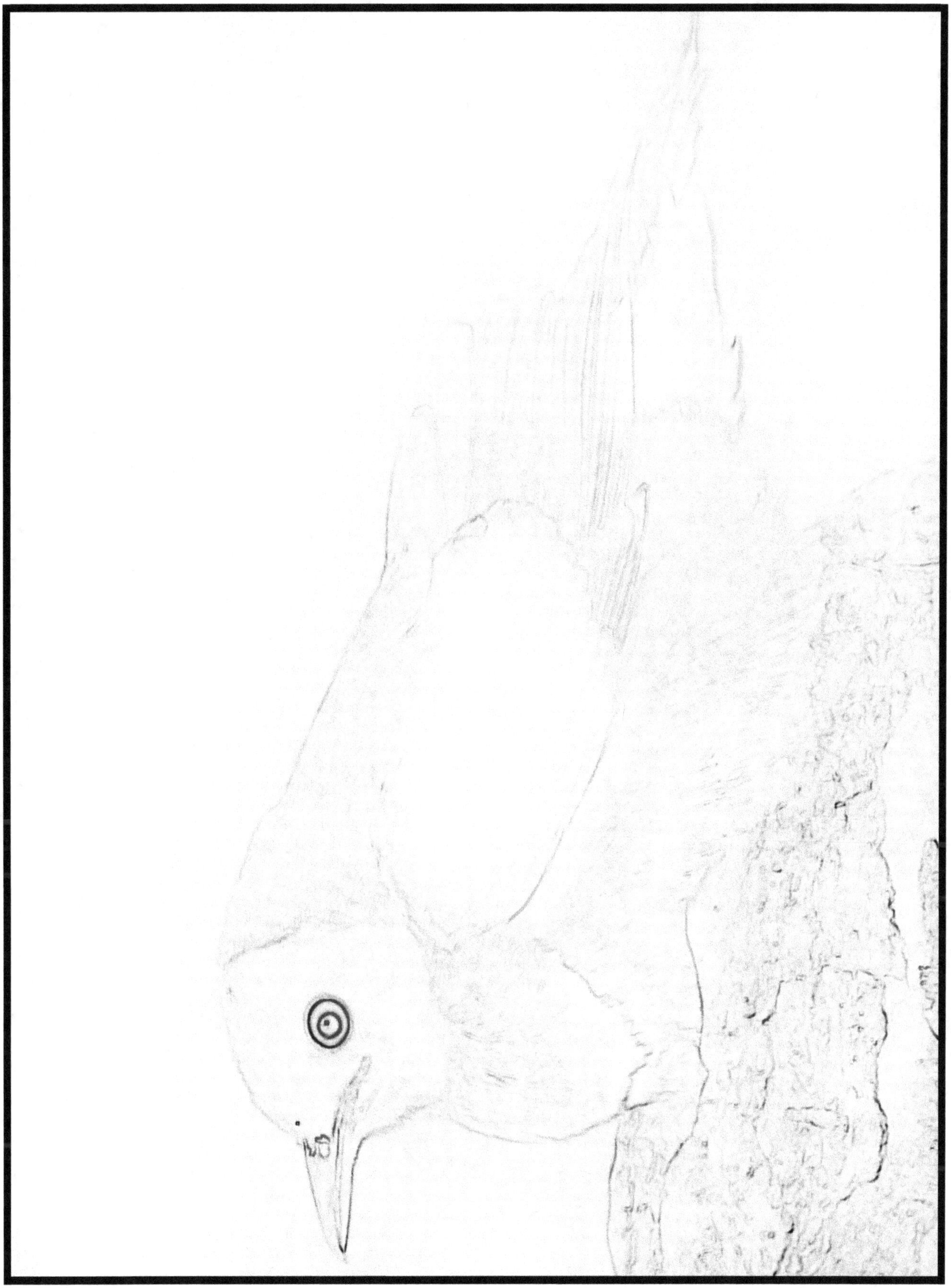

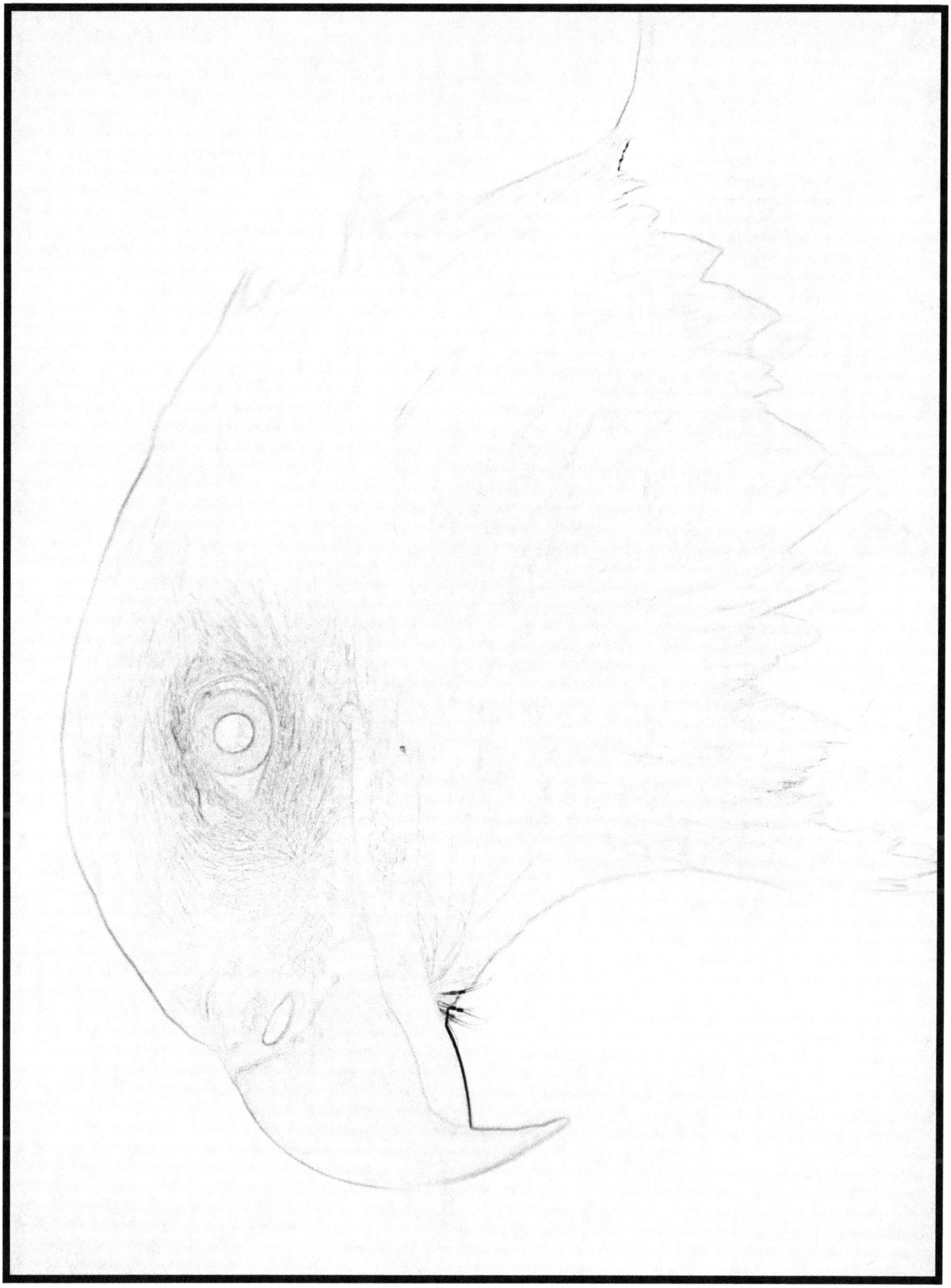

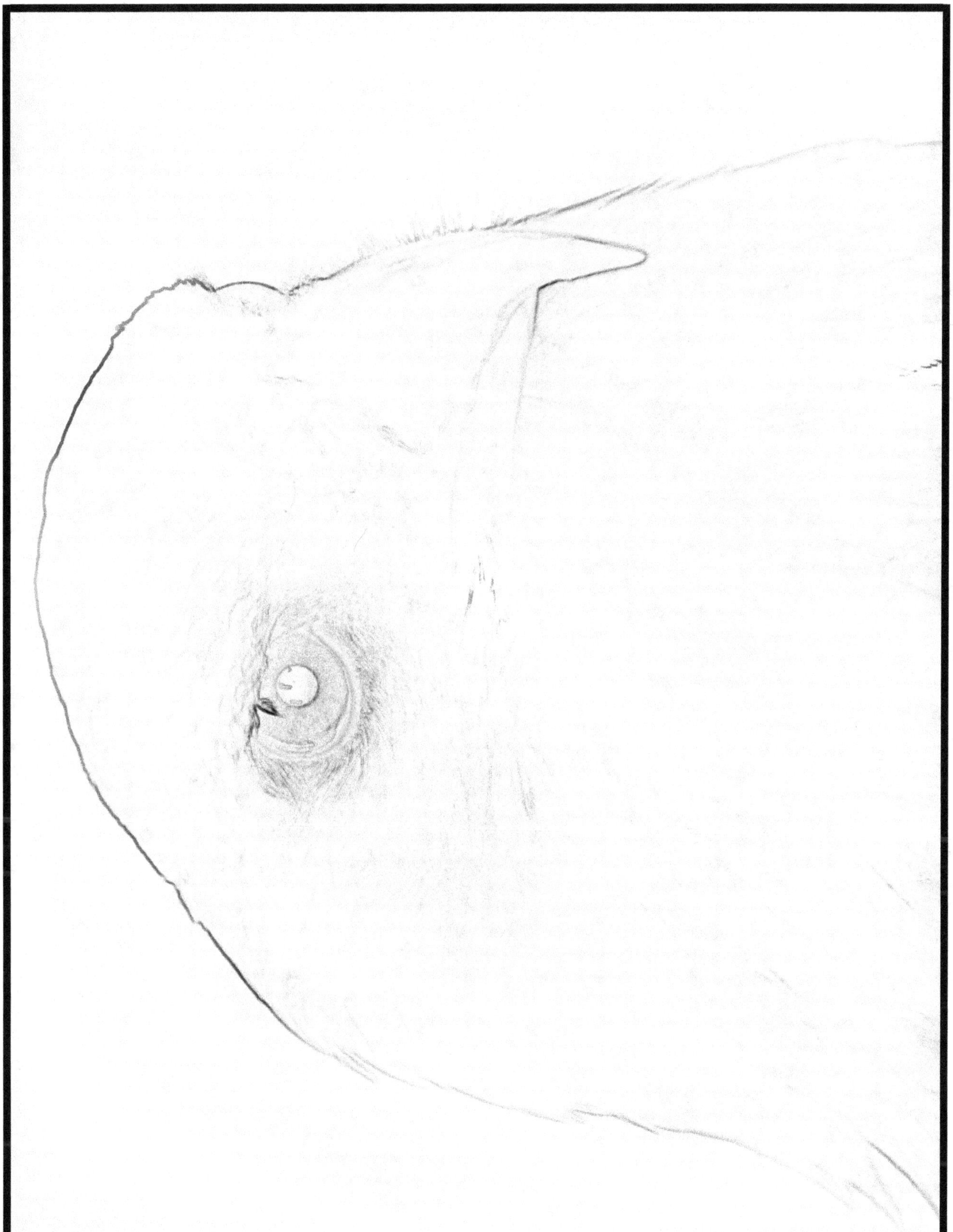

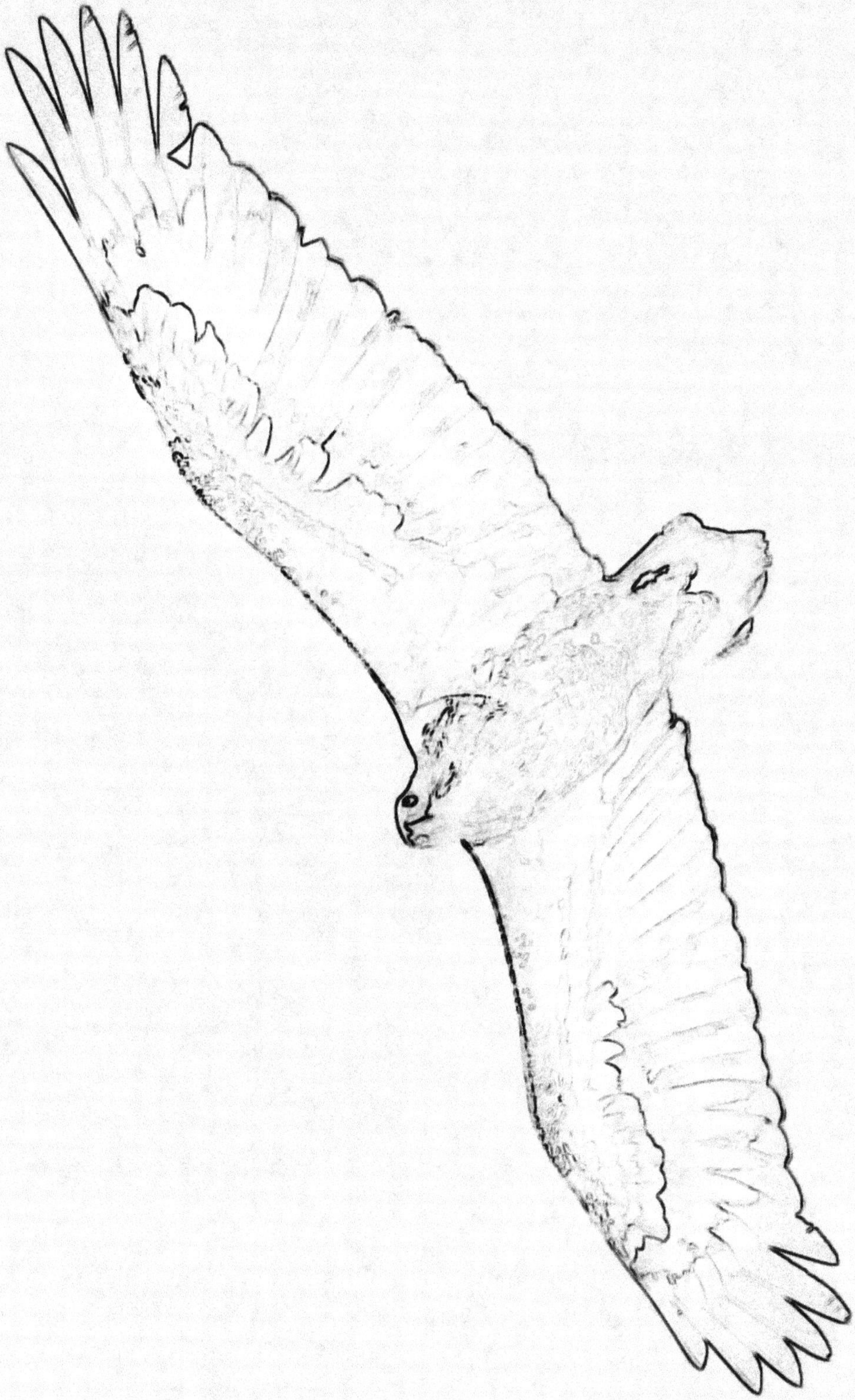

www.ingramcontent.com/pod-product-compliance
Lightning Source LLC
Chambersburg PA
CBHW081423280526
45788CB00009B/3212